GOD'S WORD, PRESENCE AND FAITHFULNESS

THE UNSHAKABLE LIFE

MERLEANNA DICK

AUTHOR

THE UNSHAKABLE LIFE

GOD'S WORD, PRESENCE AND FAITHFULNESS

The Unshakable Life: God's Word, Presence and Faithfulness
Copyright © 2023 by Merleanna Dick

Printed in the United States of America
ISBN: 979-8-218-21193-6

Published by: Joseph's Ministry, LLC
www.josephsministryllc.com

All rights reserved. This book or any portion thereof may not be reproduced or used in any manner whatsoever without the express written permission of the author except for the use of brief quotations in a book review.

P.O. Box 702211
Tulsa, OK 74170
(918) 955-0302

Unless otherwise indicated, all Scripture quotations are taken from The New King James Version of the Bible. Copyright © 1979, 1980, 1982, Thomas Nelson, Inc., Publishers.

The Scripture quotation marked NIV is taken from The Holy Bible: New International Version. Copyright © 1973, 1978, 1984 by The International Bible Society. Used by permission of Zondervan Bible Publishers.

Scripture quotations marked (KJV) are taken from the KING JAMES VERSION, public domain.

Scripture quotations are taken from the Holy Bible, New Living Translation, copyright ©1996, 2004, 2015 by Tyndale House Foundation. Used by permission of Tyndale House Publishers, Carol Stream, Illinois 60188. All rights reserved.

Scripture quotations marked (TLB) are taken from *The Living Bible*, copyright © 1971 by Tyndale House Foundation. Used by permission of Tyndale House Publishers, Carol Stream, Illinois 60188. All rights reserved.

Scripture quotations marked CSB have been taken from the Christian Standard Bible®, Copyright © 2017 by Holman Bible Publishers. Used by permission. Christian Standard Bible® and CSB® are federally registered trademarks of Holman Bible Publishers.

The Unshakable Life

Acknowledgements

First, I give honor to my Lord and Savior, Jesus Christ, without whom I would not have an unshakeable life. It is in Him that I live and can navigate and succeed in life. His written and living Word, Jesus Christ, has revolutionized and transformed me into a confident person and bold witness for Him. His daily presence empowers me to overcome the schemes of the enemy, Satan. God's faithfulness is the help I need when troubles come, which are inevitable in this life. These things have helped me become the person I am today. For this, I am eternally grateful.

I thank my husband, Ibinabo Natebo Dick, Sr., and our three children: Lydia, Tonyé, and Ibinabo, Jr., as well as our son-in-love, Kelcey. These people inspire and motivate me to pursue God the most. I will always have their prayers and support in all my endeavors.

Lastly, I thank the late Billy Joe Daugherty and his wife Sharon Daugherty, founders of Victory Christian Center, Tulsa, Oklahoma. He and this church inspired me to pursue reading the Holy Bible. As a result, I have learned to cultivate God's word, God's presence, and God's faithfulness in my life daily. I have become a fan of regular Bible reading and using a plan to help me study its books from Genesis to Revelation. I hope you will try it as well. I believe doing so will make your life unshakable.

The Unshakable Life!

The Unshakable Life is one of having God's word, God's presence, and God's faithfulness.

Focus Scripture

For the mountains shall depart, and the hills be removed; but my kindness shall not depart from you, neither shall the covenant of my peace be removed, saith the Lord that hath mercy on you. (Isaiah 54:10, KJV)

The Unshakable Life

Introduction

In this mini book, you will learn that there are three proven principles that contribute to having an unshakable life. They are important to anyone desiring to be strong in the midst of difficult situations and circumstances. The focus verse for this topic is a prophetic promise to the people of the nation of Israel. They were facing the hardships of captivity in Babylon. To get a deeper understanding of God's love and commitment to them, read Isaiah 54:1-17, NKJV. The Prophet Isaiah was speaking a word of encouragement directly from God to these people. He was letting them know that they will come back from captivity and return to God's blessings again as He had promised. God says, "For a brief moment I abandoned you, but with great compassion I will take you back. In a burst of anger I turned my face away for a little while. But with everlasting love I will have compassion on you,' says the Lord, your Redeemer." (Isaiah 54:7-8, NLT). In this reading, you will discover that an unshakable life means having God's word, God's presence, and God's faithfulness in your life. You will understand that believers in the Lord Jesus Christ will have steadfast lives through these applications, regardless of what they have to endure. Just as God has shown His faithfulness to make Israel strong through difficult times, He will do the same for you.

God's Word

His word is a lamp unto my feet, and a light unto my path.
(Psalm 119:105, NKJV)

In verse 10 of the Isaiah 54 scriptural passage, the Prophet Isaiah has a word from God to give directly to the people of Israel. You may have heard this saying, "one word from God can change your life forever." Consider these words of Jesus in this verse:

But he answered and said, "It is written, 'Man shall not live by bread alone, but by every word that proceeds from the mouth of God.'"
(Matthew 4:4, NKJV)

The first step to The Unshakable Life is being a student of God's word. There is power in the words we read and study from the Bible. When having trouble, it is important to remain attentive to hearing and obeying what God has to say to us. The temptation is to allow our emotions from the situation to distract us from the discipline of studying and meditating on scriptures. The best way to ensure that you have the discipline needed is to follow a Bible Reading Plan daily. Also, put to memory key verses that can be spoken and meditated on during times of stress and temptation.

Life difficulties come in many packages: relationship challenges, financial shortage, man-made or natural disasters, and many painful situations or circumstances that come as a part of being human. The Prophet Jeremiah makes this statement to encourage the people of Israel during their plight:

The Unshakable Life

It is of the Lord's mercies that we are not consumed because his compassions fail not. They are new every morning: great is your faithfulness. The Lord is my portion, says my soul; therefore will I hope in him.
(Lamentations 3:22-24, KJV)

      There are no greater words than those found in the Bible. God's portion can be understood as "the Lord is all I need; I can depend on Him." Making the word of God a priority in your life is the first step toward having an unshakable life. While studying the Bible every day, you will discover that life difficulties will come, but God is there with you to meet all your needs.

The Unshakable Life

God's Presence

Secondly, by being in the word of God and spending time with Him, you will experience God's presence. Jeremiah encouraged the Israelites with these words:

*And you shall seek me, and find me, when you shall search for me with all your heart.
(Jeremiah 29:13, NKJV)*

Also, Moses expresses the importance of God's presence in Exodus 33:14-16, NKJV. He writes, The LORD replied, "My Presence will go with you, and I will give you rest." Then Moses said to him, "If your Presence does not go with us, do not send us up from here. How will anyone know that you are pleased with me and with your people unless you go with us? What else will distinguish me and your people from all the other people on the face of the earth?" Take note of these few verses. God promises to go with Moses and the Hebrew people just after they had left being slaves in Egypt. It is after this that Moses asks for God's presence to be with them. Like Moses, we must acknowledge our desire for God and His presence to be with us.

In Exodus chapter 6, God lets Moses know of a more intimate relationship He wanted to have with him and the Israelite people. Up until this time, it is recorded in the Bible that Abraham, Isaac, and Jacob knew God as God Almighty or El Shaddai (Genesis 17:1, NKJV and Genesis 35:11, NKJV). Now in Exodus 6:7 (NKJV), God is saying to Moses that He wants to be Lord (Jehovah, Yahweh, or YHVH). God is saying He wants to be their God in a personal kind of way. What is the difference between God Almighty and Lord or Jehovah? The way eBible.com puts it is this, "The new name [Lord] was a more personal, intimate designation than El Shaddai [God Almighty], and indicated an intention on God's part for a relationship with humanity..." In other words, it is God's will to be close to us. Christianity advocates that through faith in Jesus, one can become very close to or be made a friend of God. The Unshakable Life is one that has a relationship with God. God – Who is not only all-powerful, is also their friend who will be present with them the same way He was with Moses. This is how it is described in the New Testament:

But now you belong to Christ Jesus, and though you once were far away from God, now you have been brought very near to him because of what Jesus Christ has done for you with his blood. (Ephesians 2:13, TLB)

The Unshakable Life is for those that have believed in Jesus Christ as their Savior. As a result, they have become close to the mighty God, who created them to be in His image and likeness. He is no longer far away, but His presence is with them in every situation of life.

The Unshakable Life

God's Faithfulness

Faith in Jesus Christ is the focal point of Christianity. Admittedly, there is an abundance of scriptures that encourage living by faith in the New Testament. Here are a few to review for yourself: Galatians 2:16 & 3:11 (NKJV), Hebrews 10:38 (NKJV), Romans 1:7-8 (NKJV), and II Corinthians 5:7 (NKJV). Faith, however, started long before Christianity was established. Take a look at this Old Testament verse:

Behold, his soul which is lifted up is not upright in him: but the just shall live by his faith.
(Habakkuk 2:4, KJV)

A study of the Bible reveals that an intimate relationship between God and His people requires faith. Christians often attribute their success to their faith in God. However, what is most important is God's faithfulness to His people. God took the first step of faith towards us when He sent Jesus Christ to redeem humanity. God continues to keep His agreements or promises. The Unshakable Life is one that realizes that they can rely on an Unshakable God who is Faithful.

God is faithful; you were called by Him into fellowship with His Son, Jesus Christ our Lord. (1 Corinthians 1:9, CSB)

In summary, The Unshakable Life comes to you when you recognize God's faithfulness to you. We must have faith in God, and that is true. Nonetheless, depending on God's faithfulness increases our ability to overcome life's struggles and trials that come to shake us. These troubles can even come to shape you and not just to shake you. To be unshakable in every situation, is to realize that God

The Unshakable Life

is faithful to you during your times of distress and disappointment. One Biblical writer says it this way:

Be strong and courageous. Do not be afraid or terrified because of them, for the Lord your God goes with you; He will never leave you nor forsake you.
(Deuteronomy 31:6, NIV)

The "them" that are trying to intimidate you do not have the power to defeat you. You have God's word, presence, and faithfulness. With all these – and His almightiness – you do not need to be afraid of anything. You are unshakable!

The Unshakable Life

Conclusion

There are three things that empower an unshakable life: God's word, God's presence, and God's faithfulness. Remember, He is Lord and longs to have an intimate relationship with you. Below are some other virtues of God to remind yourself of when you are going through difficult experiences in life:

- → He is the Lord of Your Peace
  (*Judges 6:23-24*)
- → He is the Lord Who is Present with You
  (*Exodus 6:7*)
- → He is the Lord Who Shepherds You
  (*Psalm 23:1*)
- → He is the Lord Your Provider
  (*Genesis 22:14*)

→ He is the Lord Who Gives You Victory
(*Exodus 17:15*)

→ He is the Lord Your Righteousness
(*Jeremiah 23:6*)

→ He is the Lord Your Healer
(*Exodus 15:26*)

Go live The Unshakable Life by dedicating efficient time to the study of God's word on a daily basis. Realize that God's presence is something that you cannot live without. Finally, it is not only your faith in God, but more importantly, it is God's faithfulness to you. With faith in God and by appropriating these principles, you will have all it takes to live The Unshakable Life.

About the Author

Mrs. Merleanna Dick holds a Bachelor of Science degree in Chemistry from Mississippi Valley State University and a Master of Science degree in Mathematics and Science Education from The University of Tulsa. She started her teaching career as an Adjunct Professor of Organic Chemistry at Oral Roberts University. She ended her teaching career when she retired as a high school Chemistry teacher at McLain High School in 2015.

Merleanna also worked as a Science Department Chair at McLain and has received numerous awards in her field. She received McLain's Teacher of the Year award, the Youth at Heart Champion's Heart award, and the Mentor of the Year award with the Oklahoma Foundation for Excellence.

Before retiring, Merleanna established a nonprofit organization called Education for Scholars, Inc. Her passion is to shift the mindset and achievement potential of at-risk and underserved youth. She uses education (cognitive, physical, and spiritual) to empower them to succeed in their occupational endeavors. As Executive Director, she is responsible for expanding the organization's funding, staffing, and overseeing its operations by working closely with the Board of Directors.

To learn more about the work of Education for Scholars, Inc., go to www.educationforscholars.org.

www.ingramcontent.com/pod-product-compliance
Lightning Source LLC
LaVergne TN
LVHW061606070526
838199LV00077B/7187